101 Of The World's Most Effective Pick-Up Lines

"Quand un homme se trouve vraimment au somment de la pyramide du succès, il n'est jamais seul, car aucun homme ne peut gravir d'autantiques somments sans emmener les autres avec lui

by

Keith Allen

&

Anthony Michael Ferrari

101 OF THE WORLD'S MOST EFFECTIVE PICK-UP LINES

Keith Allen

&

Anthony Michael Ferrari

Cover design & paste-up: Franz Krachtus
Cartoons & illustrations: Franz Krachtus
Layout, Editing & Design: Matthew Huijgen
Rose photography: Jay Smith
Author's photography: Josh Weintroth
Rejection Comeback # 11: Pat Chelius

For information on the above individuals, contact Kheper Publishing at the address below.

Kheper Publishing
1153 NW 51st. Street
Seattle, WA 98107

WHAT'S IN THIS BOOK
(Table Of Contents)

About The Authors v
Acknowledgments & Thanks vi
Introduction ix

1. Lines That Simply Work 13

2. The Romantic 25

3. Down With the Dirty 37

4. The Classics 47

5. Rejection Comebacks 57

6. Before The Ultimate Date 63

    Day events 66
    Evening events 67
    3 Steps to Successful Dating 68

7. Tips On The Ultimate Date 77

    Tips On The Ultimate Date 79

8. The Great Escapes 91

9. Tactics & Strategies................................ 97

Introduction 99
Tactics... 100
Keeping an open mind 100
Communication Skills 101
Manipulation 102
Don'ts.. 103
Strategies.. 104

10. The Rose 111

Order Form 125

About the authors:

Keith Allen

and

Anthony Michael Ferrari

Keith Allen and Anthony Michael Ferrari, the authors of 101 Of The World's Most Effective Pick-up Lines, have provided an entertaining, lighthearted approach to the more that ever competitive dating scene. Presented within these pages are suggestions for those who wish to obtain the ingredients of spontaneity. Moreover, this book may be used as a tool to break through the ice that had frozen over the nineties.

Both Authors have spent years researching the techniques of dating and meeting new people. From experiences observed and encountered, has been born the novel of all novelties the book of the hungry, 101 Of The World's Most Effective Pick-up Lines...

Acknowledgments & Thanks

From

Anthony Michael Ferrari

And in the sweetness of friendship let there be laughter, and the sharing of pleasures. For in the dew of little things the heart finds it's morning and is refreshed .   Gibran

I'd like to thank Keith for sharing this vision, and for his extravagant imagination which has led us into many unforget-table memories. Steven for being the fulfillment in the truest passions in my life, music and friendship. Danny for teaching me about all his knowledge of perversion. Donny for simply being the coolest guy I know. Tim for not giving a shit what I think. Jeff Buice for introducing me to the world of being inspired and writing about it. Joshua for sharing the hobby of thinking too much. Celeste for disproving the theory that distance is a girl's best friend. Jackie for keeping in touch, hopefully forever. Stephanie and Michelle for initiating me as their "goy friend." Jane for just being Jane. Jay Smith for his time and friendship ever since the church days. To some more of my friends: Sara, Wayne, Dave Wise, Steve Martin, Robert, Scott, Duane, Keith Noble, Jay Bolan. Eric C., John B., Dan Levine, Tracy, Trish and Lisa, Clark,

Jim, Mike Muller, Mark Friedman, Rich D., Gibb, Pelican Dave and the bad boys of Vomit.

Tracy for showing me that the future is exciting in perspective's I've never known, like being honest, To the lovely ladies of my best friends: Kathy, Jamie, Wendy and Bonnie.

Cheers, to all the people at New World whom with I've spent the majority of my time for the past two years. Special thanks to John Koscheka for being the only person currently saving the world Robb Smith, for the daily reminder of the torture in reality Steve Simpson, for proving my theory, you don't have to have money to be rich in love." Ileana, Scott, Barry, Fae, Jack, Dan, Jason, Cindy, Debbie, Stephanie, Amy, Kim, Tony C., Jackie, Kathy, Lindell, Margaret R., Ima, Trish and Tom Briggs. And to the rest of the people on the third floor that I don't have room to mention. These are the one's whom I've spent a many beautiful summer days inside with. To Roman, I hope to be friends with you long after our stay here at New World.

I would like to thank Jennifer Sospirato for being my teacher, my friend, and sharing the best times in my life thus far. To my parents, whom I miss, but fail to understand. Thank you to Denise Casper, for being my friend and a part of my new family forever. Thanks to my family in Arizona whom Linda, Taylor and I have recently rediscovered.

Most importantly, I sincerely give the most thanks to my sister Linda. We share the quest for an open mind. We share the calling that will lead us into a lifetime of spiritual endeavors. I love who you are. I love who you've become. And I will always love you for however you choose to be. You are my best friend in these worlds, and I thank you and Taylor for being the truest of unconditional families.

"Masturbation is nothing to be ashamed of."

Anthony Ferrari
Everyday thought

Acknowledgments & Thanks

From

Keith Allen

Thanks to Wendy for all of her love and support. The warmest possible thanks to my brother Darren for his true friendship, love and inspiration. Thanks to my parents for making me possible. To my dad Richard for his support. To M&M for your consistent hope and effort. Thanks to Anthony for the challenges, motivation and friendship. Thanks to Debbie Watson for always believing in me and supporting my dreams. Thanks to Tony, Donny, Steve and Danny for being the best friends a guy could ask for. Furthermore, thanks to all my great friends Tim, Matt Smyrnos, Linda & Taylor, Matt Thomas, Pat Chelius, Misty, Marty, Andrea, Josh, Steve Martin, Dave Wise, Kathy, Jen, Clark, Jamie, Heather, Howard, Trish and Lisa, Adam, Joey, Clark, Thomas. Jason, Doug and Mary Lou Smith, Larry and Phylus who all had some form of inspiration and support. To Jay Smith for taking the time to contribute his friendship and talent. To Noa for the rose. To Keith Noble for his masterful insight. Thanks to the old school, Donny Chelius, Tony. Steve, Craig Hering, Rick Devoe, Dumb, Bagel. Mike Muller, Mike Williams, Jerry, Bobby Watson, Jay Smith, Matt

Thomas, Shawn, Reneer, Adam, Mario, Sasha, and Adam Belgrade. You have all provided me with memories that I will forever hold close to my heart.

Thanks to Katerine Davis at MTV News, for increasing the energy, special thanks to Dr. Richard Follett for his inspiration and teaching. Another special thanks to Charlotte Doctor for challenging my beliefs and inspiring my reality. Thanks to Michael Dicora for making me a little more wise. I would like to sincerely thank all of those negative pieces of shit, who without their presence and disbelief, would none of this been possible to complete. To all who contributed their time. , effort and insight, I salute you with the greatest of respect. Most importantly, a very special thanks and well deserved credit to God, for creating my dreams and all those who believe.

"Some people are considered wise, and some people are considered otherwise."

Keith Allen

Random thought

This book is dedicated

to dreaming

and

the reality

which it stands for.

Introduction

Of course the most stereotypical thing we could do right now would be to thank you for buying our book. So, thank you for buying our book. We the authors, do not mean to sound disrespectful in any way. On the contrary, we are grateful for your contribution to the achievement of our goal. In order to understand, you'll need to be briefed. So grab your briefs and follow us into the eighties.

It was a free your mind kind of time. High school was the pond that we learned to fish in. We being Anthony Ferrari and

Keith Allen, blood brothers since childhood. It wasn't really hard to get chicks in High school. Being a surfboard shaper and a singer in a band were probably the most attractive identities we could have. Since then we've unfortunately graduated into the sea of reality, which is much different than the pond back home.

Our reasons for writing this book will soon become obvious. Our intent is to give you, the people, a lighthearted approach to the ever so competitive dating scene. How do you meet people these days? What can you say to break the ice that has frozen over the nineties?

The point is that we live in a world of pickers and choosers. At no time in history have genders ever been so competitive for control. From our experiences of these personal endeavors, we've come to the conclusion that people are quick to lower their shield to the sword of laughter.

The birth of our understanding this philosophy comes from the technique of observing, simply watching to learn.

After our teens we began our introduction to new experiences that naturally resulted in our own unique style of meeting people. It generally came from our paying close attention to the people that had come from their own ponds of sort, and somehow wound up in the same place we were. However, it was one night in particular that the light-bulb you are now reading became charged with electricity.

We began actually working on the book in the fall of nineteen hundred and ninety two. Originally, it was to only to consist of pick-up lines and pictures. Soon enough, it became obvious that the possibilities were unlimited. So be it, we began the reconstruction of our ideas. Now we approach you with the concept of strengthening your character. A world in which personality gets you things that you never imagined you'd have. This world is our world, and it's full of romantics, perverts and clowns.

While reading, you as the readers should try and pay attention to our intentions. That is to provide you with a novelty item that equips you with the confidence for success. Be warned, not all lines and suggestions will work for everybody, every time.

We suggest applying this text with your individual character to brew a soup on the menu that is too good to pass. With that in mind, we hope that you will be successful in making another person believe that your company is enjoyable and worth investigating.

As the authors we would like to disclaim any personal liability, loss or risk incurred as a consequence of the use and application, either directly or indirectly, of any advice, information or methods presented herein.

Chapter 1

Lines That Simply

Work

Lines That Simply Work

1. You have a fantastic smile, as beautiful as a Picasso... and as warm as my Jacuzzi.

Speaking of my jacuzzi...

2. I'm new in town, could I get directions to your place?

3. You with those curves and me with no brakes...

4. Would you hold it against me if I told you that you had a great body.

5.   Excuse   me...   are   you   tired?

No, why?

Because you've been running through my mind all night.

6. Pardon   me...   are   you   tired?

Yeah.

I wonder if it has anything to do with you running through my mind all night.

7. Let's say the person is wearing a name tag.

Is your name... Jamie?

It sure is!

May I call you Jamie? (as if you're asking to use their first name)

Sure, why not?

Great... what's your number?

8. Have you always been this cute, or did you have to work at it?

9. Excuse me...

I'm lost,

could you

tell me

the way to

your heart?

10. Hi, I'm writing a book of great pickup lines. What's the best one you've heard?

11. You look exactly like the person I've always wanted to meet.

12. Crazy question. Tell me the first letter in the word yellow.

Y...

Because, I thought it'd be a great way to start a conversation,

13. So, where ya from?

Around here... how about you?
Your future!

14. You know, you might be asked to leave soon. You're making the other women look really bad.

15. What's the opposite of low?

High.

Hi, nice to meetch-ya. How's it going?

16. With all the blue in your eyes, the sky has reason for being gray.

17. You don't have to believe me, but I'm from the future... and I'd like to be the first to congratulate you on being Miss America 1999.

18. You know... there's probably gonna come a point in time during the evening, when we're gonna end up giving each other a kiss good night.

Why don't we just do it now... get it over with, and go on the rest of the night feeling completely comfortable.

19. Pardon me Miss, I seem to have lost my phone number, could I borrow yours?

20. Where have you been all these beers?

21. You see my friend over there? (Point to friend who sheepishly waves from afar). He wants to know if you think I'M cute.

24. Is your boyfriend single?

22. This line is most appropriate when used at the end of a date that's gone well.

"So, can I buy you breakfast in the morning?"

"I'd like that."

"Great! Should I call you? Or... nudge you?"

23. I've got a really cute puppy at home that would love to meet you.

25. Oh, I'm doing fine! And you? (While looking at her and waiting for her to say something)

26. What are the odds of having a mutual friend that could introduce us?

✷ 27. I'd buy you a drink, but then for the first time in my life I'd be jealous of a glass.

28. I'm writing a telephone book, can I have your number?

Chapter 2

The Romantic

The Romantic

29.   Would you believe me if I told you I'm an angel and God sent me down here on a special mission just to give you a kiss?

30. I didn't know that angels could fly so low.

31. Close your eyes, I have a surprise. ....then lean over and lightly kiss her.

32. Your eyes are as deep as the ocean, save me, I'm drowning. ✳

33. Your eyes are as dark as a castle moat by midnight. Lower your drawbridge and let me cross.

34. If I planted eleven roses around you... I'd have a dozen. ✳

35. Excuse me... have you ever had a secret admire, and never found out who it was?

Yeah?

It's nice to meet you.

36. Pardon me... have you ever had a secret admirer, and never found out who it was?

No.

So you thought.

37. Has anyone ever told you that you have a magnificent smile and skin that was meant to be touched?

38. I guess the hardest thing for anyone to do is to come face to face with beauty...

I guess that's why it has taken me twenty-three years to stand here.

39. Aren't we supposed to get together for a candlelight dinner later tonight?

40. Is this seat taken as much as I am with you?

41. I was thinking about how much I'd love to be your sweater...

So that I could get as close to you as possible.

42. Excuse me... I want to tell you something, but before I do I should explain myself. A couple of months ago I found myself in a near death situation. I promised myself that if I lived through it. I would never let anything pass me by without expressing how I felt.

So... I just want to let you know, I think you're absolutely beautiful, and I hope you have a wonderful day.

43. Hi, I would usually be too intimidated to walk up to someone like you and just introduce myself...

but I know that I won't get any sleep tonight unless I do.

44. When I look into your eyes and see my reflection, there is no place I'd rather be.

45. When you rise in the morning, the sun has good reason to wake.

46. So what time does God expect you home?

47. I would love to be a tear that was born in your eyes, lived on your cheek, and died on your lips.

48. I would spend everything I have to go anywhere you were.

49. Are you as nice as you are beautiful?

50. Don't worry . . . if you kiss me, I won't turn into a frog.

Chapter 3

Down With the Dirty

3

Down With the Dirty

51. You know, I never was too good at math... like if I put you and I together, I'd get 69.

52. How do you feel about getting involved with someone who is emotionally erect?

53. Excuse me... do you have any Italian in you? Would you like some?

54. I had to swim the moat to get to you fair maiden. Would you like to see my breaststroke?

55. I've just received government funding for a four-hour expedition to find your G-spot.

56. Fuck me if I'm wrong, but you wanna kiss me.

57. There's something about you I like, if I could just put my finger on it.

58. If I were that horse, I'd rather you mounted me without the saddle.

59. My... you have gorgeous hair, but it would look more lovely in my lap.

60. If you could use one fruit to describe yourself what would it be?

I don't know, why?

Because I picture you as a banana, just begging to be peeled and eaten.

61. Excuse me... your legs are just my size. Do you mind if I try them on?

62. It's been a busy day. Why don't you lay back and I'll fill you in.

63. Do you believe in the hereafter?

Then you know what I'm here after.

64. Hi, I'm superman... and you look great naked!

65. Is that a short skirt you're wearing, or just a wide belt?

66. I bet you're like
M&M's... you'd melt in my mouth, not in my hands.

67. You should be glad I'm not a Viking. You would
have been ravaged and plundered by now.

68. Just being in the same room with you is a tease.

66. Voulezvous vous coucher avec moi ce soir? 'Voolayvoovoo shay ahhvay muah say suaw' (Would you like to go to bed with me tonight?)

67. How would you like to join me in some math? We'll add you and me, subtract our clothes, divide your legs, and multiply!

68. You smell delicious.

69. Let's have a party and invite your pants down.

70. You look like you could use some protein in your diet.

71. My name is _____, remember it, you'll be screaming it all night.

72. I'm an organ donor, need anything?

Chapter 4

The Classics

4

The Classics

77.   Can I see your tan lines?

78. Hey... didn't we go to different schools together?

79. I'd really like to lick orange brandy out of your navel.

80. What's your sign?

81. You know what would look absolutely great on you tonight?

Me.

82. Do you know any good pick-up lines?

83. Print up cards that say: "Smile...." on the front, and "....if you want to sleep with me!" on the back. Then watch your victim try to hold back her smile.

84. Excuse me, what's your name... or can I just call you mine?

85. Your father was a thief, he stole the stars from the sky and put them in your eyes.

86. Smile, I'm single.

87. What do you say I cook you dinner, you cook me breakfast... and in between we eat?

88. Wanna go down to the beach and watch the submarine races?

89. What's a fair maiden like you doing in a dungeon like this?

90. Your teepee or mine?

91. You probably recognize me from my underwear ads.

92. Excuse me... haven't we taken a shower together before?

93. Your father must have been in construction, because you're built with a great foundation.

94. God, you smell great. What is that you're wearing?

95. I've been noticing you not noticing me.

96. Haven't I met you someplace before?

97. Do fries come with that shake?

98. (Check her shirt tag)... Just as I thought, made in heaven!

99. So, what color is your underwear?

100. If I had a good line right now, I'd use it.

101. Did you know it's my birthday?

Chapter 5

Rejection Comebacks

Rejection Comebacks

1. Is it just the light in here, or are you as stunning as you think you are?

2. Would you like to dance?

No!

Come on, don't be picky... I wasn't.

3. Excuse me... would you like to dance? No!

No... I said you look fat in those pants.

4. Excuse me... would you like to dance? No.

No...I said you're too fat to dance. Get off the floor or I'll call the fat police.

5. You know what? You and I really have something in common.

What?

We both think you're hot.

6. You know... I was standing over their thinking to myself that this girl looks like she could use a friend right now.

But now that I'm closer, I can see that your friend is distance.

7. Will you marry me?

Marry you?

Marry me?

you're scary to me.

8. Let me ask you this.

How many drinks do you think it would take to make you look good enough.

9. You know, that drink really brings out the blood shot in your eyes.

10. Too bad... I would love to pick you up, but I don't think I can.

11. Do your eye's bother you?

No. Why?

Because they bother me.

Chapter 6

Before The Ultimate Date

Before The Ultimate Date

More than 100

of the World's Most Effective

Date Idea's

The following pages show a listing of all the date ideas that you can try with your new date!

These date ideas are classified under day events and evening events:

Day Events

1. Nature hikes
2. Bike rides (mountain or street)
3. Water parks
4. The beach or lake
5. Bungee jumping
6. Sky diving
7. Horse back riding
8. Rock climbing
9. Miniature golf
10. Flying
11. Hot air balloon rides
12. Helicopter tours
13. Hay rides
14. Fishing
15. Go see a matinee movie
16. Get stoned
17. Rent a movie
18. Watch a porno
19. Fun park/Carnival
20. Museums
21. Fly a kite
22. Go to the park
23. Go sailing
24. The Zoo
25. Have a picnic
26. Workout
27. Favorite sport
28. Fishing
29. Row boating
30. Arcade
31. Whale watching
32. Day concert
33. Magic shop
34. Nude beach
35. Sight seeing
36. Camping
37. Go for a drive
38. Play catch
39. Rollerblading
40. Swimming
41. Observatory
42. Bowling
43. Wine Tasting
44. Driving range
45. Golfing
46. Day spa
47. Make-overs
48. Fancy lunch
49. Shooting
50. Used book store

Evening Events

51. The beach
52. Star gazing
53. Bowling
54. Miniature golf
55. Play pool
56. Dancing
57. Coffee house
58. Home cooked meal
59. Elegant dinner
60. Twister
61. Limousine travel
62. Helicopter tours
63. See a concert
64. The Drive-in
65. Some wine and the moon
66. Get stoned
67. Rent a good movie
68. Fun park/Carnival
69. Watch a porno
70. Play/Opera
71. Blind folded fruit tasting
72. Go-cart racing
73. Watch the sunset
74. Watch the sunrise
75. Bubble bath
76. Photos
77. Karaoke
78. Window shopping

79. Play Monopoly
80. Play favorite sport
81. Poetry readings
82. Arcade
83. Crash a wedding
84. Hot tubbing
85. Gambling
86. Strip poker
87. Sex shop
88. Submarine races
89. Wine tasting
90. Get a tattoo
91. Night spa
92. Inspiration point
93. Roller skating
94. Crash a party
95. Circus
96. Sporting event
97. Comedy show
98. See a new movie
99. BBQ
100. Skinny dipping
101. Hide n seek
102. Bonfire
103. Sushi
104. Re-runs of Cheers
105. Mall strolling

Three Steps to Successful Dating

If there's one time you should really try and remember the little things, it's a first date. To assist you in doing so, we will break this part of the chapter down into three sections: "Before the Date," "During the Date," and, The Conclusion." In the beginning of each section we will provide you with some tips that should make a difference in your first impression.

Then at the end of each section we'll equip you with a couple of suggestions to help impress upon your date that you've really been thinking ahead.

You obviously can't use everything we suggest every time. Although, you should get used to the idea of preparation, which in turn should transform experiences into memories.

Before the Date

1. Flowers; This is traditional but effective. Your objective is to impress upon your date that you value their company.

Before the Date (cont'd)

2. Music:
Set a mood by preparing music that you and your date will listen to in the car.

3. Cologne/Freshener:
Make sure the car has a nice scent. If you smoke, make sure to leave enough time in between your last cigarette and picking up your date. This is to allow the inside of your car some time to air out. Even if they smoke, it's nice to give a first impression of freshness.

4. Fresh breath:
Don't be a yuck mouth.

5. Reservations/Plans:
Prepare an open itinerary so your date flows smoothly. Sometimes spontaneity can be your best friend, so be flexible. In other words, don't over plan.

6. Directions:
Know where you're going.

7. Gas and Money:
It's smart to bring a credit card for emergencies.

8. Condoms:
Be smart!

9. Confidence:

The most important thing to do before you pick up your date, is to feel good about yourself and what you have to offer.

10. This book:

Use it as a tool for reference.

Hints/Suggestions

1. Find out before hand where your date originally grew up. Spend some at the library researching some local trivia that will make your date feel at home.

2. Pack a blanket and candles in the trunk of your car. This is to provide you with the option to be romantic at the right time.

During the Date

1. Decision making:

"What should we do?" When this question arises, don't procrastinate. Simply ask if they have a preference, if they don't, then make the decision. Trust your instincts.

2. Be honest.

If you anticipate seeing this person again, don't fabricate the truth. Lying will just cause you headaches down the road. Make the truth interesting, even if it isn't.

3. Compliments:

Refer to "Manipulation" within the chapter, "Tactics & Strategies."

4. Conversation:

Refer to "Communications Skills" within the chapter "Tactics & Strategies."

5. Be courteous, and always open their door.

6. Personal hygiene, check the following:

— Your teeth
— Your nose
— Your breath after meals and before kissing
— Your zipper
— Your hair
— Your posture
— And most importantly, check your attitude at the door

7. Find out what they prefer to eat, and order it for them.

8. Don't begin eating before they do.

Hint/Suggestions

1. Position an arrangement of flowers on the passenger seat of your car. Don't forget to open their door. This will act as a potent surprise on which your date will begin.

2. Inform your date that you need to use the restroom. Find the server, and politely ask if they would do you a small favor. If they are hesitant, go on to hint that it would benefit their gratuity if they play along. Simply ask them to approach your table informing you and your date that someone in the restaurant has just complimented on what a great couple you make.

The Conclusion

1. Get in the door:
Attempt to be invited in for a drink, and/or conversation.

2. Second date:
If you sense there is a mutual attraction, suggest a second date. If you're not sure, don't ask. Wait for them to dissolve or confirm your doubt.

3. First kiss:
Trust your instincts.

4. Sex:
Be safe!

Hints/Suggestions

1. If there is no mention of a second date, you should call them the following afternoon leaving a "thinking about you" message on their machine. If they call you back within the day, they are most likely interested in seeing you again. If not, refer to the chapter, "Tactics & Strategies," and try again.

2. Suggest to your date that it would be nice to stop for coffee. If they agree, stop at the nearest store and purchase a can of your favorite instant.

3. To make a classy exit, leave a paper rose in a setting that won't reveal itself until you've gone.

And in closing

We hope this section acts as an effective checklist for your successful dating experiences. You should refer to it whenever necessary: before the date, during the date, and at the conclusion.

To further enhance your perspective on dating, read the following chapter, "Tips On The Ultimate Date."

Chapter 7

Tips On The Ultimate Date

Tips On The Ultimate Date

Tips On The Ultimate Date

Getting to know someone, or redefining your feelings for someone, demands time to explore character and personality. For many years now, people have utilized the information they have observed to create the nicest possible surroundings for the one they admire.

During the process of creating this book, we researched the methods of romance in their rawest form. These are not just words in a book that sound nice. Rather, they are the relived experiences that proved effective to say the least.

We investigated the true response. Meaning, we searched for what happens when two people who are attracted to each other, are alone with each other. What do they say that sounds nice in private, but would otherwise sound foolish in the presence of others.

As you read through our suggestions, try to imagine yourself involved with the scenario. What would you change about the tip to be more accommodating to your own situation. We hope that this chapter will assist you in expanding your own ideas.

These tips for the ultimate date are designed to work individually or combined. They interact nicely to provide you with various choices.

We hope that the result of you applying our ideas to whatever situation arises, is that of true success.

#1.

There is something about nature and good company that sparks the brightest of connections. Even if your date has been a long time companion, this tip should bring back, or magnify, those intense feelings of happiness just being together.

First, inform your date that the two of you will be going for a hike (or mountain bike ride, if accessible). Secretly pack a bottle of favorite wine (don't forget a corkscrew if you bring wine) or Champagne into some sort of easily carried bag or backpack. If neither of you drink alcohol, then we suggest using a non-alcoholic sparkling apple cider, which can be found in almost any grocery store. Furthermore, most sparkling ciders' are packaged similar to Champagne which gives rise to a romantic touch.

You should also bring along glasses to drink from. If accessible, use crystal or glass to add a sense of class. To avoid any packed glass from clinking around, giving your surprise away, securely wrap each piece with a towel so that they are separated from each other.

If for some reason your date asks why you're bringing a pack, reply that you've brought a jacket in case it gets cold. If you live in a warm climate, or it just happens to be hot, reply that you've brought along some food in case you get hungry.

Part of the preparation is choosing a location. Find a nice romantic place that is set away from distractions. Such places can be found by creeks and streams as well as mountains and forests. If none of these places are accessible, then use your imagination and think about the places that you're familiar with.

Once you reach your secret destination, suggest to your date that it would be nice to relax there for a minute. Initiate casual conversation for a few minutes.

Then ask your date what their definition of true romance is. Once a reply has been given, discuss it until they ask you what your definition is. If for some reason they don't ask, bring it up yourself.

Once this occurs, you are now ready for the kill. A reasonably smooth way to perform this surprise is to first discuss your definition of true romance. Be sure not to go overboard, unless appropriate. You may want to mention things like flowers, Champagne, wine and good company. Mention the romance of surprises and how nice they can be.

Immediately after expressing these thoughts, look for the prettiest flower around. If there aren't any flowers, find the prettiest something around and put it in place of the flowers for this example.

Another good suggestion, is to make a paper rose while

talking. Refer to the chapter within this book entitled, "The Rose." This works well, but make sure to act as if you're fidgeting with a piece paper until the rose is obviously formed. If you do choose to use this angle, be sure that you practice making the rose before the date. In other words, know how to make it fairly well so that it makes a better impression.

Instruct your date to take notice of the flower, or pretty something. Then say, "this is for you." Next, pull the glasses and bottle from your pack and say something to this effect, "and this toast is to us and the true meaning of romance." You can say this before or while you open the bottle so that there isn't a lull in between. These words and the appearing bottle compliment each other nicely for the climax.

#2.

This second ultimate date tip could and should be applied with number one. Especially if there is some sort of special occasion like a birthday or anniversary. If there is no special occasion, or it's a hope date, meaning you hope to win this persons heart, be sure that it would be appropriate first. Find out if it's something that would upset your date, instead of happily surprising them. If all is go, you should be very pleased with your results from this tip.

There are two great ways to set this one up. First, if your date works at night, plan on going for the hike or bike ride a couple of hours before he or she is scheduled to be at work.

Go to your date's manager, supervisor, partner or colleague and explain your situation. Ultimately, your goal is to persuade them to let your date miss work. People love romance and usually warm up to it, so be polite yet persuasive if necessary.

Generally if they agree to give your date the time off, they will often assist in one more key ingredient to this plan.

Politely ask, beg if necessary, if he or she will speak into one of those hand held tape recorders saying something to this effect, "Hi _____ (your date's name), this is so and so, happy whatever. Guess what, you don't have to come in to work tonight. Just relax and have fun."

If your date works during the day, or their boss won't let them off, then secretly ask one of their friends or family members to make plans with your date at night on a weekend. Use that friend or family member to record the message instead of the boss or partner. Instruct them to cancel their plans on the tape recording while everything else remains the same.

Play the recorded message just before you expose the bottle of wine or Champagne on the hike or ride. Do this by saying something like, "speaking of romance, that reminds me." Then play the tape and proceed with additional tips.

Remember that all tips may be altered as you see fit. Although, try not to stray to far from these suggestions, they have all been tested & resulted in great success.

#3.

Traditionally, the dinner has been a symbolic event that marks the boundaries of an official date. In a modern world such as ours, evolution has provided us with a few more creative options than in the past.

If finances are tight then dig out your cookbook. If you don't have one, borrow one from a friend or family member. If none of these options are available to you, then watch a morning home show, or look in a home-related magazine for a delicious sounding recipe.

After your hike or bike, suggest to your date that they relax, and take their time to get ready without being rushed. Be sure to tell them you're going for a nice dinner so they know what to wear. If they ask where you'll be going, simply reply that it's a surprise that will only be revealed when it arrives. If they are extremely persistent, or you like this better, reply that you're going to a cozy little place that reminds you of home.

When you return to pick up your date, arrive with some kind of flowers. We suggest either a spring bouquet, or red roses. It doesn't really matter if the flowers come from a neighbor's yard or a flower shop. Flowers seem to be a great symbol of admiration and respect, use them whenever you can.

People love to be complimented. Find a certain thing about this person that you think they may be self-conscious of. For example, compliment them on their hair or noticeable piece of clothing or jewelry.

The next step is to prepare the meal at either your residence or a friend's. We suggest bribing one of your friends to dress up and act like a server from the French Riviera. Have your friend act as a private waiter who serves the meal and clears the plates. Your friend's attitude should resemble the soft spoken obedience of a butler, "yes sir, no m'am.

You should have some sort of conversational beverage waiting for your arrival. We suggest wine or Champagne.

In addition, you may also want to include the appropriate music. If finances will allow, we suggest hiring a private musician(s) for cocktails and dinner. Instruments that provide a touch of romance are the violin, saxophone, clarinet, flute, harp, and acoustic or nylon guitars.

If having dinner out sounds more appealing, then try to find out the name of your date's favorite restaurant. You can do this by asking one of their friend's or family members. If you know your date, then try to remember a place you may have heard them mention. Someplace they would love to check out. If this information is not available, then select a place you think they would enjoy.

For the rest of the evening you should enjoy each other's

company discovering new things, or reviving fond memories.

BONUS TIP FOR NUMBER THREE

To spice it up a bit, hire a limosine for the evening. Other than just driving in them, limousines can be a great prop involved with surprising someone.

The key is to make everything unexpected up to the last second. For example, instead of bringing flowers to the door, leave them in the limo. This way, your date will be even more blown away when they get inside the car.

Instruct your limo driver to park out of plain view. In addition, be certain the driver knows the directions to all the places you plan on going. If the driver has to ask while your date is with you, it may force you to reveal upcoming surprises. Besides, it's a more luxurious experience when the driver doesn't need to ask for directions.

After the details are set, then go to your date's door. If you're invited in, do so, but remember not to leave the upcoming surprise waiting to long. If your date is running late, be patient but remind them of your special dinner reservation.

As you're leaving the residence, say to your date, "would you like to drive, or should I?" Whatever their response is, reply, "why don't we take the limo!" This should be said just as the limosine becomes visible. The power of this surprise is all in the timing.

If you need a distraction for the limosine because your date is suspicious of surprises, show up earlier than the limo so you won't keep it waiting during this detour.

Go inside and talk for an accommodating amount of time about things that come up. Somehow, fit in to the conversation that your car isn't running that well, and either you or they may have to drive their car. The point is to provide your date with something that will distract their imagination from thinking you hired a limosine.

If that's not good enough, take it one step further. Try to arrange with the driver a time in which you can page him. Most limo drivers carry a pager so this shouldn't be a problem.

Your driver should wait down the street from a designated spot he will meet you. When your driver gets the page, it should be a signal that you are leaving the residence and will be driving by in just a couple of minutes.

As soon as the driver spots you passing by, he should begin to follow you. As soon as you see him in your rear view mirror, pull over and pretend as though you forgot something. When your date asks what it is that you forgot, reply, "another surprise."

At this point, the limosine should either pull up next to you, or you should say something like "no I didn't, its right behind us."

Another great way to do this, is to pull into a gas station and say your car sounds funny. Inform your date that your mechanic recommended not to drive when you heard this noise. Tell your date not to worry, you're going to call a cab and take care of your car later.

Go to the closest phone and page your limo driver. When he pulls up tell your date that the cab has arrived.

#4.

Tip number four is the most adventurous of these ultimate date tips. Although intense and exciting, this tip has a few requirements. First, a little money. Second, the accessibility of its ingredients. Third, the desire to provide somebody with a memory that will last a lifetime.

In addition, the success of this date tip depends on your geographic location, and whether or not your date likes to fly.

Most cities have companies that specialize in romantic services. We suggest using a helicopter company that provides romantic tour packages. These packages can be extremely glamorous to wild and adventurous. The package we suggest usually consists of limosine service with an escort. Elegant dining on the top floor of a tall building, provided they offer sky dining in your area.

After dinner, you and your date will be escorted to the stairwell leading to the roof by your escort/limo driver and maître 'd. Just noticing the people watch you and your date being ushered to the roof is a thrill in itself.

The moment intensifies as you enter the designated stairwell and journey upward one flight to the roof. At this point your date should be wondering what is happening, but not yet completely aware of what is about to happen.

Within a matter of seconds, as you reach the half way mark in the stairwell, it will become obvious that a helicopter awaits you. This will be apparent due to the magnificent sound of rotary blades spinning in preparation to depart on a magical flight.

As the roof access door opens you will both be blown away by the sight and sound of a jet helicopter flashing it's brilliant lights. The wind caused by the spinning blades raises the excitement as you are escorted to the chopper door.

Once inside the helicopter, you will most likely wear head phones so that you can communicate with each other as well as with the pilot.

After being cleared for departure you will notice the increased level of jet power as you are lifted from the roof into the open sky. As you fly by the restaurant you dined at, you will most likely notice the same people who watched you ushered to the roof, watching you fly away.

Usually these flights are about forty-five kilometers long; lasting about twenty to thirty minutes. Amongst the many beautiful sights, you should be able to witness fairy tale lights, landmarks, and much more.

The flight ends as you gently land within feet of your limosine, which was driven to this location while you where eating dinner. From this point you and your date are driven home in the comfort of your own private limo to indulge in whatever you please.

Remember, not all helicopter companies provide tours like this one. I have experienced this exact tour in Los Angeles with a nation-wide company called Heli-USA. In fact, they were absolutely incredible. Their service and professionalism were outstanding. If you would like to call them for a reservation or information about their available tours, call (800) 443-5487. They may even be able to provide you with a reference for your area if you live outside their nearest location.

Some other great suggestions for this kind of date range from hot air balloon rides to yacht tours. Check your local listings for one of these companies and investigate availability and price.

If your date and/or you prefer not to fly, check into horse carriage rides. Whether it be city park horse tours, or small town hay rides, they can be extremely romantic and relaxing.

In conclusion, if you plan to perform tips one through four combined in one day, you should expect to spend about eight hundred dollars. Our tips start at about six dollars and go up from there.

In addition, we would like to remind you about making all the necessary arrangements and reservations well before the date. This is to save you from experiencing any avoidable difficulties.

We understand that you may want to mix and match ideas. They will all work together, or separate if applied with sincerity and imagination. If you lack these two qualities then follow our suggestions and you should be fine.

Be aware, that it doesn't matter which tip, or combination of tips you use. Expensive or inexpensive, separately or together, they should be successful provided there is a mutual desire to be together. Before spending large amounts of money, we suggest making sure there is at least some romantic potential, if indeed that is what you're after. Most importantly, go with the flow, have fun, and make the best of everything.

Chapter 8

The Great Escapes

8

The Great Escapes

You're out on a date that doesn't seem to be going as well as you would have liked. You are now confronted with a choice. To either continue or discontinue the date.

Most people continue because they are afraid to speak the truth, resulting in their discomfort. Unless there is some educational reason, continuing with a date that is undesired is, in our opinion, wrong. Time is too precious.

Besides, the other person may be thinking the same thing about you. You should be confident, open, and do with your night what you wish. The best thing to do is be honest and straightforward. Although effective, this method may be cold and hurtful.

In search of discovering a way to save the other person's feelings from being dashed on the rock's of reality, we developed a few easily applied steps known as 'The Great

Escapes." Remember to use these tips within the scope of your own personality. Moreover, have fun altering any suggestions to better fit your own situation.

Escape # 1

If you own a pager be sure to bring it along, especially if you're on a first date. Have a friend page you with a 911 following their number at a specific time. This is in case your date needs some form of verification. If a pager is not available, instruct your friend to have you paged by the maître 'd. of the establishment. You now have an opportunity to get away for a minute to collect your thoughts, take a needed break, etc. If there is a phone nearby, call your friend to see what else in going on so that you can make alternative plans.

After rejoining your date, simply explain that a serious dilemma has arisen. Express your apologies as well as inform the person that this dilemma requires immediate attention and you'll need to go. The date's over, and you are now free.

When and if he/she asks about seeing each other again, tell them to call you. When and if they call, explain that you have rejoined with your ex, and would like to be friends. Unless of course you feel otherwise.

Escape # 2

If you've been set up on a blind date, try this. When making the plans, persuade your date to meet you at your residence.

If you disapprove when they arrive at your door, ask them immediately who they're there to see. When they reply your name, respond with, "Oh... he/she left an hour ago. Was he/she expecting you?"

At this point you have taken on the roll of your roommate. Play it from there.

Escape # 3

When on a date that seems to be going well on one side (the other person's), try this.

Tell your date that you're sorry, but you just can't do it. You thought you could, but you just can't. When they ask what it is you can't do, reply, "Go out, I mean... I'm married."

If you predict that you may have to use this one, be prepared. Bring along a ring and/or prepare some information about your married life. You may even go so far as to act scared, informing your date that your spouse is sitting in the next booth. If you're not in a restaurant, then inform your date that your spouse is in the general vicinity. Then get up and leave quickly.

Escape # 4

This is the old, "get sick trick." If you're on a date that is obviously ill fated, inform this person early that you're feeling a little under the weather.

About an hour later, relate that your condition has progressively gotten worse. Express regret. But you feel as though it would be beneficial to your health if you went home and got some sleep.

This will require some acting on your part to be pulled off effectively. So let us help with our ten quick suggestions for a believable excuse:

1. Migraine

2. Out late the night before before the date.

3. Hung over

4. You feel the flu coming on

5. Cramps

6. Unsettled stomach/Bad food

7. Stress

8. Emotional phone call

9. Back pain

10. Headache

Escape # 5

When all else fails, go to the rest room, and never go back.

Bye-Bye...

Chapter 9

Tactics & Strategies

Tactics & Strategies

__Introduction__

A question of strategy may arise when dating or socializing. A good strategy may be the key element in one's own success. The problem is that most people naturally observe their friends or some respected hero at work. From this observation they absorb certain moves or lines with the expectation of having equal success to that of their instructors. Sometimes they may, but more often than that, they will fail.

Strategy is not one particular move or line. It isn't something you can directly learn from us, or anyone else for that matter. Rather, a good strategy is a combination of tactics, personal character, comfort, sincerity and a little trial and error.

This chapter is designed to provide you with the basic ingredients of certain tactics and strategies. More than presenting you with words that are magic, you benefit from the basic concepts.

Please keep in mind that we are not equipped psychologists or therapists. Rather, we have only our opinion regarding some of the most successful angles of social techniques.

They may not all agree with your standards, or comply with the expectations of being a new form of communicating. The intent and purpose of this chapter is to merely highlight some of the diverse aspects of social interaction. Such aspects include, communication skills, keeping an open mind, manipulation and so on.

So pull up a chair, open your mind, and take from our advice what you wish.

Tactics

Keeping an Open Mind

Keeping an open mind is a great tool for any situation. This ability allows you to view others with no strings attached. We all have wants, needs and desires to be seen as attractive by others, but these hopes can often kill what we wish for others to see in us. For instance, if you're talking with someone whom you're attracted to, you'll most likely shift your personality towards satisfying what you perceive to be his or her expectations. Since you're not a mind reader, you're left only to guess what it is this person likes. Ultimately, you may misrepresent yourself by leading the other person to be un-attracted, or attracted, to someone you're not.

The right attitude to have in this situation is not to concentrate on fulfilling this person's expectations. Rather, you should concentrate on your own expectations, and whether or not this person truly meets them. Whether they're attractive or not, research their character for qualities other than their appearance. In the process of doing this you should keep an open mind. Don't be cocky, but act as if though you're remaining open to what this person can offer you.

People need change in their lives. By keeping an open mind and talking with someone whom you've never met, you stand to learn about things you could have otherwise never known. This action could bring about change, enhancing the quality of your character.

The point is that keeping an open mind unlocks many doors both physically as well as intellectually. A lot can be learned from all kinds of people, regardless their sex, size, shape or color. An unimportant piece of trivia learned from someone you talk to, could be the thing that creates interest in you from the one you truly desire.

Obtaining an open mind does take a little time and effort. Although, once you achieve this socially powerful tool, you will surely discover a talent that is rewarding in many arenas of life.

Communication Skills

Verbal communication provides one with many choices. There are tones, styles, and many other factors that create character and technique. It seems that all these choices, combined with human emotion, provide most with a sense of confusion when talking to unfamiliar people.

You are always interacting with different people, strangers or not. Some may have power or seniority over you. Others may be your peers. Regardless of their personal status with you, they are separate individuals who will almost all interpret your words or message, differently from each other.

There are a few rules you should follow when talking with someone one-on-one. First, people love to hear the sound of their own name. Using someone's first name, or respected title, is personable and during a conversation helps to lower their guard. Besides that, it helps to implant someone's name in to your head for the next possible time you meet.

Second, it is a well-tested theory that a person who's considered a great conversationalist allows their audience to speak about seventy percent of the time. The key strategy is to ask questions related to what they offer as well as to things they seem to enjoy.

A great tool to equip yourself with, to truly gain verbal success, is to be multi-dialectical. Simply stated, this means different forms of speaking around different people.

For example, when I went bungee jumping with some friends, I commented on the, "balls" that it took to do. If I was to speak with an older group of folk, I might mention the guts involved. If I were conversing with a group of scientists, I would refer to the intestinal fortitude, which simply means guts or balls euphemistically.

The key point to take from this bit, is that people interpret the meaning of certain words differently. This is not to say that you should change who you are, or what you're saying. Rather, let your attitude and message change the impression of others.

Manipulation

Manipulation is another tactic that can be very effective when applied gently, and in the correct manner. For example, the next time you meet with someone, pay attention to something about this person that they may not like about themselves. Compliment them on whatever it is that they appear to be conscious of; their hair, make-up, clothes, physique, car, voice, and so on.

This tactic will bring attention to your manner and admiration. Furthermore, it will make someone feel good, resulting in their possible interest in remaining with you to continue receiving this security. In other words, you may have lowered someone's guard, making it easier for you to receive whatever it is you want.

A wise man once told me, "The secret to earning respect is doing things for others without getting caught; you'll be amazed with the results." For us that means making a difference in the life of another without being concerned with the reward or attention it may provide. In fact, experimenting with this philosophy has uncovered the most gratifying results ever.

People seem to be much more pleased and grateful when, and if, they do discover who it was that, "Santa Claused" a favor. Small things are large gifts. Secrecy is the key.

These tactics are designed to enhance the Strategy section within this chapter. You should apply them with sincerity and personal technique. Most people can sense whether or not someone is being honest about their intentions. Some choose to play along, but most people run for cover when they feel preyed upon.

Don'ts

Flashback for a moment and reminisce. Recall the last time you met someone new who had mutual attraction to you. Remember the last time you were alone with someone and stayed up all night talking. It's a great feeling to have, although confusing at times, especially for those who are slow to lower their guard.

The successful, or ultimately successful attitude to have in this situation, is to not lie about anything. Even if you're only out to get laid, your mouth will get you in trouble somehow, some way, someday. For example, what if for some unimaginable reason, you end up falling in love with this person who thinks you're last week's lotto winner. Even worse, what if the person you meet next month, whom you really like, lives next to the person you lied to. You'll feel like shit and probably lose the person you really enjoy spending time with.

Another great way to self-destruct your long and/or short term dating results is to brag about you or your friends' lives. Women are especially turned off by this easily detectable expression of a bullshit character. Ultimately, the loss is yours as your ego is thrashed upon the rocks of truth and reality.

Strategies

Whether you prefer to call them games or strategies,

there will always be people who play them to win the lust or love of another. Whether it is their attitude or your game, we have provided you with some effective tips.

"Knowledge is only as powerful as it's persistence"
Keith Allen

#1

Playing hard to get is either a failure or complete success, so be cautious. The ones who are often the most vulnerable to this strategy are those who appear to be insecure.

The technique with this strategy is to seem friendly, but have no burning interest. Commonly, when people feel as if they're being ignored, they long for acceptance by paying more attention to the people who acknowledge them the least.

Occasionally direct your attention elsewhere, while remaining friendly and intrigued. This should create any potential interest from your opponent.

The next move is to exchange phone numbers. Remember, if you give someone reason to believe that you're an interesting person worth investigating, getting their number is a cinch. Moreover, it's not the number, it's how you use it.

Don't call them, unless they don't have your number, and then only after three days of not hearing from them. You might think that if they haven't called you in three days, then what's the point? Well, it may just be that a further crucial step is necessary to draw that person into the clenching fists of your desire. After three days have gone by, it's now time for that first bonding phone conversation. The one where you talk for hours sharing your views on sex, family, politics and so on. You make each other laugh and smile.

Even after the first bonding conversations, phone calls

should be limited. You should never assume that after these events you're automatically, "in there." You still need to create a sense of demand to fully claim victory. Never call twice in one day, or more than once every other day. You should only need to do this for about a week or two. After this point you should be more in touch with where you stand.

Ultimately your goal is to sweep them off their feet. Some are hard to do this to, but if you hang up the phone leaving them with the impression that you're a cool person, you're on your way.

Make sure they have your phone number if you still haven't heard from after three more days, be persistent and call them.

If this happens and you still haven't made plans, ask them if they would like to do something on a specific night that you choose. When the plans are set, cancel them the morning or night before. The reason for this is to cause them to sense a fear of loss. Similar to the tactic a salesman uses when attempting to persuade a buyer that he only has "one left," and someone else is on their way over to pick it up. The result of effectively applying this tactic is that your opponent may want you more than they originally thought. Although, this can also be a very crucial moment, so go easy. Reschedule the plans during the same phone conversation with the sincerity of making it up to them. Prepare a date along the lines of what we suggest in the "Before The Ultimate Date" Chapter 6. Use your insight to plan something effective, and not stifling.

If they call you, return their phone calls. Don't always be so quick to call them back, and don't always sound interested. Occasionally when talking with them, express that you need to go, due to other plans. If they ask what it is your doing, say; "I'm going out with a friend." This response should provoke their curiosity. Furthermore, it's usually not long after this point that they will come to you about your feelings for each other.

This may all seem difficult to pull off, but believe us, these steps, combined with the ability to tailor to your situation, will create curiosity and further interest from your opponent. People want what they can't have.

#2

Appearing to only want friendship is another risky, but effective, back door strategy. There are many ways to manoeuver through this method of entry. The two that seem to be the most effective are the "secret sex partner" and the "casual supportive friend." The potencies of these methods are at their highest levels when your opponent has just recently parted from their former relationship.

Along with Captain Steubing (from the "Love Boat" TV-series) and raw attraction, sex may be the true action responsible for people falling in love. The relevant point is that good friends, the best of friends, build a certain level of love, trust, and caring. Without sex they still have strong feelings for each other. Alternatively, two people who posses the same bond of friendship and caring, and who also have sex, have feelings that surpass the bond of a strictly platonic friendship.

The strategy involved with achieving a sexual friendship is to first become friends. When you meet someone new, the approach should be non threatening.

Get into an interesting conversation, and before it's over attempt to exchange phone numbers. Your attitude should be indicative to the desire of just being good friends. You do this by applying the communication techniques mentioned earlier and talk about things friends talk about. The aim is to direct your audience to think of you as someone they would like to be friends with.

Once you go through the motions of getting to know this person fairly well as a friend, maybe after meeting and talking a few times, feel out their personality to see if they would be adventurous and wild. In other words, find out if they wanna get in bed.

You do this by having a wild conversation beginning with views on sex. If the conversation elevates to an erotic level, propose slanted questions regarding secret relationships, founded upon sex. Be careful though, if they catch wind of your intentions, the deal is off. This is not to say that you wouldn't have true genuine feelings for this person. Rather, your primary goal is more to "touch" the genuine feelings of this person.

Probe the issue of sex and friends. If you sense they may be attracted to you; light-heartily joke around and suggest the possibilities of you two playing together. Be sure not to be obnoxious. Rather, take on a new tone in your voice. One that implies comfort. Depending on the response to this particular conversation, the ball is now in the confidence of your own hands.

#3

Being a warm understanding, yet fun friend, is often the best way to attract someone you really enjoy spending time with. It could be someone you have known and always had a crush on, or it could be someone you've been friends with, and now want more. It could be someone attractive whom you just met. Whatever the situation, the strategy is essentially the same.

You start with casual conversation. Become friends, find out what it is they really enjoy in life. If you already know, find out more. Your attitude should be caring but non threatening, especially if this person is in a relationship, on the rocks or not.

Be supportive by talking with this person about issues in their life. Offer advice when you can. Establish a true sense of fun and comfort around yourself. Be careful though and check the vibe. The last thing you want is to let the other person fall into the harsh reality that your friendship is too good to ruin.

You stop this from happening by playing a little hard to get after a few weeks of bonding. Be charming and polite, but don't go overboard with the friendly stuff. Don't let the other person dictate the time you spend together. The reason for doing this is to create a small level of demand.

Once this is present, suggest a casual dinner date for just the two of you. Keep it light-hearted and fun. If you're a guy, bring flowers. If you're a girl, don't bring a thing. The reason for this is that guys' may get spooked by a gift or card. If it's a guy who would like an award, still don't give it to him. It might make him want you more.

If you drive to wherever it is you're going, listen to music you both like. If you and your date like to smoke pot, get stoned and have a blast. If you and your date like to drink, get a few cocktails before or at dinner. The whole point is not to intoxicate your friend or yourself. Rather, it is to relax the mood and encourage fun whenever you two are together, with or without intoxication.

After dinner, take a walk somewhere that is non-distracting and scenic: the beach, park, forest, country road, and so forth. Someplace comfortable to talk.

You can try one of two methods once you feel the time is right, First, look into their eyes and passionately kiss. When the kiss pauses, you should say, "I've always wondered what that would feel like." If you get rejected, apologize for being so forward; but you "just had to touch their lips." Whether you choose to say that or not, you should continue with the second method (the second method may be used in place of the first one all together if you wish).

Second, begin talking about your relationship with this person. Mention things like how much fun you're having. This is to instill positive thoughts around you. Next, mention that your feelings are growing stronger and that you would like to spend more time together. Without seeming nervous or insecure. Just flow with the conversation you have, or are about to open.

If things go well, then apply the first method just mentioned, kiss passionately on the lips.

If you get rejected, either take it like whatever gender you are, or tell them not to be picky because you weren't.

Conclusion

Dating and being single have their pros and con's. We have attempted to give you some of our opinions on the subject in hope of assisting you in some way.

Remember that our advice is not always going to work. What will always work is you and your mind, unless there is some unfortunate accident. You will always be able to refer to your instincts, which are in fact the key elements to the success of your endeavors and our suggestions. Have fun, be safe, and be successful.

Chapter 10

The Rose

The Rose

How to make a Paper Rose

...and score Big!

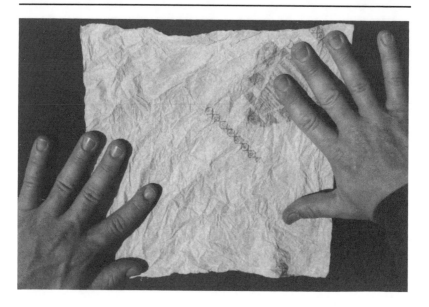

1. For the best results, use a normal bar napkin or tissue paper.

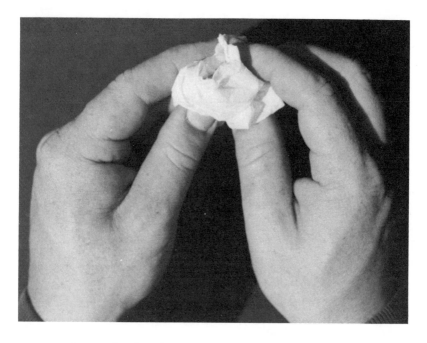

2. Crumple the paper into a ball. This will add character to the final product by providing a ruffled look.

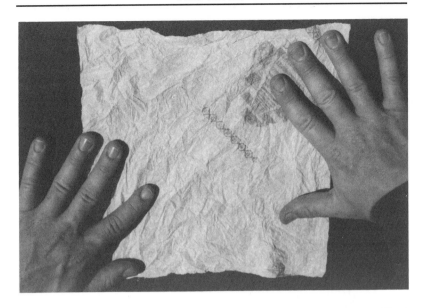

3. Being careful not to rip the paper, unfold the ruffled ball. Make sure all corners are flat.

4. Pick a corner, while lightly wetting your index finger and thumb to provide a better grip. Begin rolling the paper toward your body.

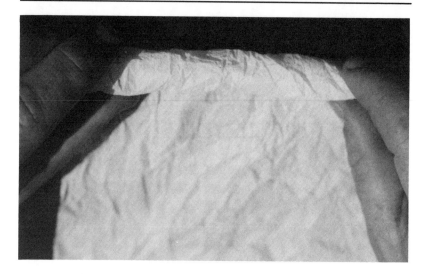

5. While continuing to roll the paper towards you, concentrate on gradually making each roll a little bigger than the one before.

6. To add fullness to the bud of your rose, allow the last couple of inches to be really loose. If you look at instruction number seven's picture, you'll notice the contrast between the middle and the end.

7. Securely cradle the roll in your hand. The top of the roll should now resemble the bud.

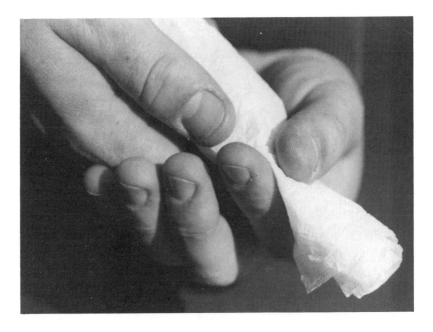

8. Place your dry index finger and thumb about two inches from the top, lightly pinching them together. If using paper larger than a napkin, be sure to adjust the size of the bud accordingly.

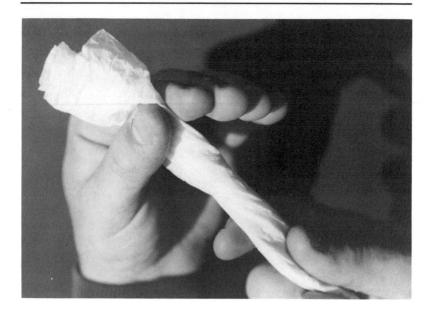

9. While maintaining this finger position, lightly pull down and twist with your free hand.

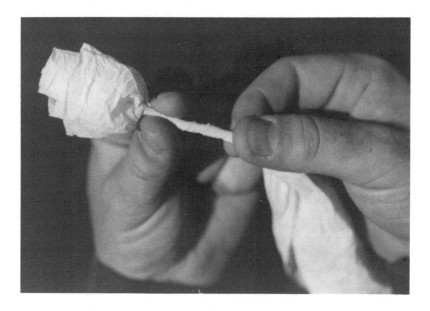

10. Twist the paper below the bud fairly tight. This will later become the stem of your rose. Be careful not to twist and pull too tight, the paper may rip.

11. Continue twisting the stem until you are two to three inches from the bud.

12. Locate the bottom edge of the paper on the stem and separate it.

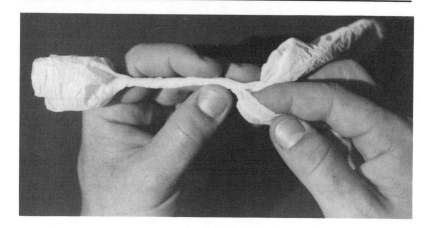

13. Run your finger up the edge until you reach the twisted area of the stem.

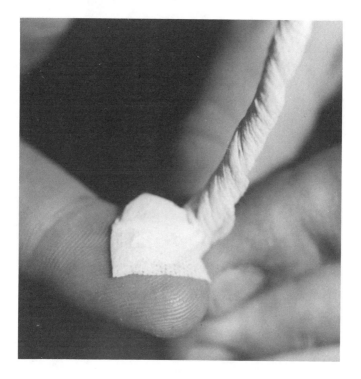

14. Use your index finger to shape a leaf by pulling out a small area of the napkin that hasn't been twisted yet. Place your index finger and thumb below this area and twist a couple of times.

15. Once a leaf is formed, continue to twist and pull to the end of the stem.

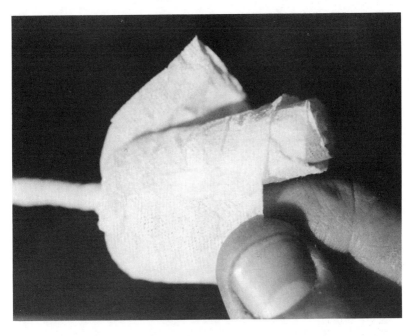

16. You should now fine-tune the rose by tightening the stem and better shaping the bud. Do this with the tip of your index finger. Be careful, the paper rips easily!

17. Notice the tight stem and the full round base of the bud.

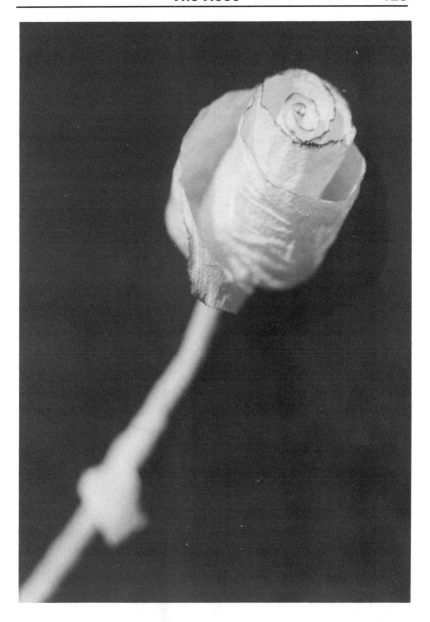

18. You now have your final product. To add a little flair you may carefully burn the edges. The paper burns easy, so run the flame by quickly while blowing out any area that catches on fire.

Have fun and Good Luck!

The End